THE TROJAN WOMEN

OF EURIPIDES

TRANSLATED INTO ENGLISH RHYMING VERSE WITH EXPLANATORY NOTES BY

GILBERT MURRAY

A Digireads.com Book
Digireads.com Publishing
16212 Riggs Rd
Stilwell, KS, 66085

The Trojan Women
By Euripides
Translated by Gilbert Murray
ISBN: 1-4209-2732-9

Please visit *www.digireads.com*

THE TROJAN WOMEN

In his clear preface, Gilbert Murray says with truth that *The Trojan Women*, valued by the usage of the stage, is not a perfect play. "It is only the crying of one of the great wrongs of the world wrought into music." Yet it is one of the greater dramas of the elder world. In one situation, with little movement, with few figures, it flashes out a great dramatic lesson, the infinite pathos of a successful wrong. It has in it the very soul of the tragic. It even goes beyond the limited tragic, and hints that beyond the defeat may come a greater glory than will be the fortune of the victors. And thus through its pity and terror it purifies our souls to thoughts of peace.

Great art has no limits of locality or time. Its tidings are timeless, and its messages are universal. *The Trojan Women* was first performed in 415 B.C., from a story of the siege of Troy which even then was ancient history. But the pathos of it is as modern to us as it was to the Athenians. The terrors of war have not changed in three thousand years. Euripides had that to say of war which we have to say of it to-day, and had learned that which we are even now learning, that when most triumphant it brings as much wretchedness to the victors as to the vanquished. In this play the great conquest "seems to be a great joy and is in truth a great misery." The tragedy of war has in no essential altered. The god Poseidon mourns over Troy as he might over the cities of to-day, when he cries:

"How are ye blind,
Ye treaders down of cities, ye that cast
Temples to desolation, and lay waste
Tombs, the untrodden sanctuaries where lie
The ancient dead; yourselves so soon to die!"

To the cities of this present day might the prophetess Cassandra speak her message:

"Would ye be wise, ye Cities, fly from war!
Yet if war come, there is a crown in death
For her that striveth well and perisheth
Unstained: to die in evil were the stain!"

A throb of human sympathy as if with one of our sisters of to-day comes to us at the end, when the city is destroyed and its queen would throw herself, living, into its flames. To be of the action of this play the imagination needs not to travel back over three thousand years of history. It can simply leap a thousand leagues of ocean.

If ever wars are to be ended, the imagination of man must end them. To the common mind, in spite of all its horrors, there is still something glorious in war. Preachers have preached against it in vain; economists have argued against its wastefulness in vain. The imagination of a great poet alone can finally show to the imagination of the world that even the glories of war are an empty delusion. Euripides shows us, as the centre of his drama, women battered and broken by inconceivable torture—the widowed Hecuba, Andromache with her child dashed to death, Cassandra ravished and made mad—yet does he show that theirs are the unconquered and unconquerable spirits. The victorious men, flushed with pride, have remorse and mockery dealt out to them by those they fought for, and go forth to unpitied death. Never surely can a great tragedy seem more real to us, or purge our souls more truly of the unreality of our thoughts and feelings concerning vital issues, than can The Trojan Women at this moment of the history of the world.

FRANCIS HOVEY STODDARD.
May the first, 1915.

INTRODUCTORY NOTE

Judged by common standards, the *Troädes* is far from a perfect play; it is scarcely even a good play. It is an intense study of one great situation, with little plot, little construction, little or no relief or variety. The only movement of the drama is a gradual extinguishing of all the familiar lights of human life, with, perhaps, at the end, a suggestion that in the utterness of night, when all fears of a possible worse thing are passed, there is in some sense peace and even glory. But the situation itself has at least this dramatic value, that it is different from what it seems.

The consummation of a great conquest, a thing celebrated in paeans and thanksgivings, the very height of the day-dreams of unregenerate man—it seems to be a great joy, and it is in truth a great misery. It is conquest seen when the thrill of battle is over, and nothing remains but to wait and think. We feel in the background the presence of the conquerors, sinister and disappointed phantoms; of the conquered men, after long torment, now resting in death. But the living drama for Euripides lay in the conquered women. It is from them that he has named his play and built up his scheme of parts: four figures clearly lit and heroic, the others in varying grades of characterisation, nameless and barely articulate, mere half-heard voices of an eternal sorrow.

Indeed, the most usual condemnation of the play is not that it is dull, but that it is too harrowing; that scene after scene passes beyond the due limits of tragic art. There are points to be pleaded against this criticism. The very beauty of the most fearful scenes, in spite of their fearfulness, is one; the quick comfort of the lyrics is another, falling like a spell of peace when the strain is too hard to bear (cf. p. 89). But the main defence is that, like many of the greatest works of art, the *Troädes* is something more than art. It is also a prophecy, a bearing of witness. And the prophet, bound to deliver his message, walks outside the regular ways of the artist.

For some time before the *Troädes* was produced, Athens, now entirely in the hands of the War Party, had been engaged in an enterprise which, though on military grounds defensible, was bitterly resented by the more humane minority, and has been selected by Thucydides as the great crucial crime of the war. She had succeeded in compelling the neutral Dorian island of Mêlos to take up arms against her, and after a long siege had conquered the quiet and immemorially ancient town, massacred the men and sold the women and children into slavery. Mêlos fell in the autumn of 416 B.C. The *Troädes* was produced in the following spring. And while the gods of the prologue were prophesying destruction at sea for the sackers of Troy, the fleet of the sackers of Mêlos, flushed with conquest and marked by a slight but unforgettable taint of sacrilege, was actually preparing to set sail for its fatal enterprise against Sicily.

Not, of course, that we have in the *Troädes* a case of political allusion. Far from it. Euripides does not mean Mêlos when he says Troy, nor mean Alcibiades' fleet when he speaks of Agamemnon's. But he writes under the influence of a year which to him, as to Thucydides, had been filled full of indignant pity and of dire foreboding. This tragedy is perhaps, in European literature, the first great expression of the spirit of pity for mankind exalted into a moving principle; a principle which has made the most precious, and possibly the most destructive, elements of innumerable rebellions, revolutions, and martyrdoms, and of at least two great religions.

Pity is a rebel passion. Its hand is against the strong, against the organised force of society, against conventional sanctions and accepted Gods. It is the Kingdom of Heaven within us fighting against the brute powers of the world; and it is apt to have those qualities of unreason, of contempt for the counting of costs and the balancing of sacrifices, of recklessness, and even, in the last resort, of ruthlessness, which so often mark the paths of heavenly things and the doings of the children of light. It brings not peace, but a sword.

So it was with Euripides. The *Troädes* itself has indeed almost no fierceness and singularly little thought of revenge. It is only the crying of one of the great wrongs of the world wrought into music, as it were, and made beautiful by "the most tragic of the poets." But its author lived ever after in a deepening atmosphere of strife and even of hatred, down to the day when, "because almost all in Athens rejoiced at his suffering," he took his way to the remote valleys of Macedon to write the *Bacchae* and to die.

G. M.

THE TROJAN WOMEN

CHARACTERS IN THE PLAY

THE GOD POSEIDON.

THE GODDESS PALLAS ATHENA.

HECUBA, *Queen of Troy, wife of Priam, mother of Hector and Paris.*

CASSANDRA, *daughter of Hecuba, a prophetess.*

ANDROMACHE, *wife of Hector, Prince of Troy.*

HELEN, *wife of Menelaus, King of Sparta; carried off by Paris, Prince of Troy.*

TALTHYBIUS, *Herald of the Greeks.*

MENELAUS, *King of Sparta, and, together with his brother Agamemnon, General of the Greeks.*

SOLDIERS ATTENDANT ON TALTHYBIUS AND MENELAUS.

CHORUS OF CAPTIVE TROJAN WOMEN, YOUNG AND OLD, MAIDEN AND MARRIED.

The Troädes was first acted in the year 415 B.C. "*The first prize was won by Xenocles, whoever he may have been, with the four plays Oedipus, Lycaon, Bacchae and Athamas, a Satyr-play. The second by Euripides with the Alexander, Palamêdês, Troädes and Sisyphus, a Satyr-play.*"—AELIAN, *Varia Historia,* ii. 8.

THE TROJAN WOMEN

The scene represents a battlefield, a few days after the battle. At the back are the walls of Troy, partially ruined. In front of them, to right and left, are some huts, containing those of the Captive Women who have been specially set apart for the chief Greek leaders. At one side some dead bodies of armed men are visible. In front a tall woman with white hair is lying on the ground asleep.
It is the dusk of early dawn, before sunrise. The figure of the god POSEIDON is dimly seen before the walls.

POSEIDON. [1]
    Up from Aegean caverns, pool by pool
    Of blue salt sea, where feet most beautiful
    Of Nereid maidens weave beneath the foam
    Their long sea-dances, I, their lord, am come,
    Poseidon of the Sea. 'Twas I whose power,
    With great Apollo, builded tower by tower
    These walls of Troy; and still my care doth stand
    True to the ancient People of my hand;
    Which now as smoke is perished, in the shock
    Of Argive spears. Down from Parnassus' rock
    The Greek Epeios came, of Phocian seed,
    And wrought by Pallas' mysteries a Steed
    Marvellous [2], big with arms; and through my wall
    It passed, a death-fraught image magical.
      The groves are empty and the sanctuaries
    Run red with blood. Unburied Priam lies
    By his own hearth, on God's high altar-stair,
    And Phrygian gold goes forth and raiment rare
    To the Argive ships; and weary soldiers roam
    Waiting the wind that blows at last for home,
    For wives and children, left long years away,
    Beyond the seed's tenth fullness and decay,
    To work this land's undoing.
                         And for me,
    Since Argive Hera conquereth, and she
    Who wrought with Hera to the Phrygians' woe,
    Pallas, behold, I bow mine head and go
    Forth from great Ilion [3] and mine altars old.

When a still city lieth in the hold
Of Desolation, all God's spirit there
Is sick and turns from worship.—Hearken where
The ancient River waileth with a voice
Of many women, portioned by the choice
Of war amid new lords, as the lots leap
For Thessaly, or Argos, or the steep
Of Theseus' Rock. And others yet there are,
High women, chosen from the waste of war
For the great kings, behind these portals hid;
And with them that Laconian Tyndarid [4],
Helen, like them a prisoner and a prize.

    And this unhappy one—would any eyes
Gaze now on Hecuba? Here at the Gates
She lies 'mid many tears for many fates
Of wrong. One child beside Achilles' grave
In secret slain [5], Polyxena the brave,
Lies bleeding. Priam and his sons are gone;
And, lo, Cassandra [6], she the Chosen One,
Whom Lord Apollo spared to walk her way
A swift and virgin spirit, on this day
Lust hath her, and she goeth garlanded
A bride of wrath to Agamemnon's bed.

[He turns to go; and another divine Presence becomes visible in the
    dusk. It is the goddess PALLAS ATHENA.]

    O happy long ago, farewell, farewell,
Ye shining towers and mine old citadel;
Broken by Pallas [7], Child of God, or still
Thy roots had held thee true.

PALLAS.

                 Is it the will
Of God's high Brother, to whose hand is given
Great power of old, and worship of all Heaven,
To suffer speech from one whose enmities
This day are cast aside?

POSEIDON.

His will it is:
Kindred and long companionship withal,
Most high Athena, are things magical.

PALLAS.

Blest be thy gentle mood!—Methinks I see
A road of comfort here, for thee and me.

POSEIDON.

Thou hast some counsel of the Gods, or word
Spoken of Zeus? Or is it tidings heard
From some far Spirit?

PALLAS.

For this Ilion's sake,
Whereon we tread, I seek thee, and would make
My hand as thine.

POSEIDON.

Hath that old hate and deep
Failed, where she lieth in her ashen sleep?
Thou pitiest her?

PALLAS.

Speak first; wilt thou be one
In heart with me and hand till all be done?

POSEIDON.

Yea; but lay bare thy heart. For this land's sake
Thou comest, not for Hellas?

PALLAS.

I would make
Mine ancient enemies laugh for joy, and bring
On these Greek ships a bitter homecoming.

POSEIDON.

Swift is thy spirit's path, and strange withal,
And hot thy love and hate, where'er they fall.

PALLAS.
A deadly wrong they did me, yea within
Mine holy place: thou knowest?

POSEIDON.
I know the sin
Of Ajax [8], when he cast Cassandra down....

PALLAS.
And no man rose and smote him; not a frown
Nor word from all the Greeks!

POSEIDON.
And 'twas thine hand
That gave them Troy!

PALLAS.
Therefore with thee I stand
To smite them.

POSEIDON.
All thou cravest, even now
Is ready in mine heart. What seekest thou?

PALLAS.
An homecoming that striveth ever more
And cometh to no home.

POSEIDON.
Here on the shore
Wouldst hold them or amid mine own salt foam?

PALLAS.
When the last ship hath bared her sail for home!
   Zeus shall send rain, long rain and flaw of driven
Hail, and a whirling darkness blown from heaven;
To me his levin-light he promiseth
O'er ships and men, for scourging and hot death:
Do thou make wild the roads of the sea, and steep
With war of waves and yawning of the deep,
Till dead men choke Euboea's curling bay.

So Greece shall dread even in an after day
My house, nor scorn the Watchers of strange lands!

POSEIDON.
I give thy boon unbartered. These mine hands
Shall stir the waste Aegean; reefs that cross
The Delian pathways, jag-torn Myconos,
Scyros and Lemnos, yea, and storm-driven
Caphêreus with the bones of drownèd men
Shall glut him.—Go thy ways, and bid the Sire
Yield to thine hand the arrows of his fire.
Then wait thine hour, when the last ship shall wind
Her cable coil for home!

[Exit PALLAS.]

How are ye blind,
Ye treaders down of cities, ye that cast
Temples to desolation, and lay waste
Tombs, the untrodden sanctuaries where lie
The ancient dead; yourselves so soon to die!

[Exit POSEIDON.]

* * * * *

The day slowly dawns: HECUBA wakes.

HECUBA.
Up from the earth, O weary head!
    This is not Troy, about, above—
    Not Troy, nor we the lords thereof.
Thou breaking neck, be strengthenèd!
Endure and chafe not. The winds rave
    And falter. Down the world's wide road,
    Float, float where streams the breath of God;
Nor turn thy prow to breast the wave.

Ah woe!... For what woe lacketh here?
    My children lost, my land, my lord.
    O thou great wealth of glory, stored
Of old in Ilion, year by year

We watched ... and wert thou nothingness?
  What is there that I fear to say?
  And yet, what help?... Ah, well-a-day,
This ache of lying, comfortless

And haunted! Ah, my side, my brow
  And temples! All with changeful pain
  My body rocketh, and would fain
Move to the tune of tears that flow:
For tears are music too, and keep
A song unheard in hearts that weep.

[She rises and gazes towards the Greek ships far off on the shore.]

O ships, O crowding faces
  Of ships [9], O hurrying beat
  Of oars as of crawling feet,
How found ye our holy places?
Threading the narrows through,
  Out from the gulfs of the Greek,
Out to the clear dark blue,
  With hate ye came and with joy,
And the noise of your music flew,
  Clarion and pipe did shriek,
As the coilèd cords ye threw,
  Held in the heart of Troy!

What sought ye then that ye came?
  A woman, a thing abhorred:
  A King's wife that her lord
Hateth: and Castor's [10] shame
  Is hot for her sake, and the reeds
Of old Eurôtas stir
With the noise of the name of her.
  She slew mine ancient King,
  The Sower of fifty Seeds [11],
    And cast forth mine and me,
  As shipwrecked men, that cling
    To a reef in an empty sea.

Who am I that I sit
　　Here at a Greek king's door,
Yea, in the dust of it?
　　A slave that men drive before,
A woman that hath no home,
　　Weeping alone for her dead;
　　A low and bruisèd head,
And the glory struck therefrom.

[She starts up from her solitary brooding, and calls to the other Trojan
　　Women in the huts.]

O Mothers of the Brazen Spear,
　　And maidens, maidens, brides of shame,
　　Troy is a smoke, a dying flame;
Together we will weep for her:
I call ye as a wide-wing'd bird
　　Calleth the children of her fold,

To cry, ah, not the cry men heard
　　In Ilion, not the songs of old,
That echoed when my hand was true
　　　On Priam's sceptre, and my feet
　　　Touched on the stone one signal beat,
　　And out the Dardan music rolled;
And Troy's great Gods gave ear thereto.

[The door of one of the huts on the right opens, and the Women steal
　　out severally, startled and afraid.]

FIRST WOMAN.
　　　　　　　　　[Strophe I.]
　　How say'st thou? Whither moves thy cry,
　　　Thy bitter cry? Behind our door
　　　We heard thy heavy heart outpour
　　Its sorrow: and there shivered by
　　　　Fear and a quick sob shaken
　　From prisoned hearts that shall be free no more!

HECUBA.

Child, 'tis the ships that stir upon the shore....

SECOND WOMAN.

The ships, the ships awaken!

THIRD WOMAN.

Dear God, what would they? Overseas
Bear me afar to strange cities?

HECUBA.

Nay, child, I know not. Dreams are these,
    Fears of the hope-forsaken.

FIRST WOMAN.

Awake, O daughters of affliction, wake
And learn your lots! Even now the Argives break
    Their camp for sailing!

HECUBA.

Ah, not Cassandra! Wake not her
  Whom God hath maddened, lest the foe
Mock at her dreaming. Leave me clear
  From that one edge of woe.
O Troy, my Troy, thou diest here
  Most lonely; and most lonely we
  The living wander forth from thee,
    And the dead leave thee wailing!

[One of the huts on the left is now open, and the rest of the CHORUS come out severally. Their number eventually amounts to fifteen.]

FOURTH WOMAN.

[Antistrophe I.]

Out of the tent of the Greek king
  I steal, my Queen, with trembling breath:
  What means thy call? Not death; not death!
They would not slay so low a thing!

FIFTH WOMAN.
O, 'tis the ship-folk crying
To deck the galleys: and we part, we part!

HECUBA.
Nay, daughter: take the morning to thine heart.

FIFTH WOMAN.
My heart with dread is dying!

SIXTH WOMAN.
An herald from the Greek hath come!

FIFTH WOMAN.
How have they cast me, and to whom
A bondmaid?

HECUBA.
Peace, child: wait thy doom.
Our lots are near the trying.

FOURTH WOMAN.
Argos, belike, or Phthia shall it be,
Or some lone island of the tossing sea,
Far, far from Troy?

HECUBA.
And I the agèd, where go I,
A winter-frozen bee, a slave
Death-shapen, as the stones that lie
Hewn on a dead man's grave:
The children of mine enemy
To foster, or keep watch before
The threshold of a master's door,
I that was Queen in Troy!

A WOMAN TO ANOTHER.
[Strophe 2.]
And thou, what tears can tell thy doom?

THE OTHER.
>The shuttle still shall flit and change
>Beneath my fingers, but the loom,
>>Sister, be strange.

ANOTHER (wildly).
>Look, my dead child! My child, my love,
>The last look....

ANOTHER.
>>>Oh, there cometh worse.
>A Greek's bed in the dark....

ANOTHER.
>>>God curse
>That night and all the powers thereof!

ANOTHER.
>Or pitchers to and fro to bear
>>To some Pirênê [12] on the hill,
>>Where the proud water craveth still
>Its broken-hearted minister.

ANOTHER.
>God guide me yet to Theseus' land [13],
>>The gentle land, the famed afar....

ANOTHER.
>But not the hungry foam—Ah, never!—
>Of fierce Eurotas, Helen's river,
>To bow to Menelaus' hand,
>>That wasted Troy with war!

A WOMAN.
>>>[Antistrophe 2.]
>They told us of a land high-born,
>>Where glimmers round Olympus' roots
>A lordly river, red with corn
>>>And burdened fruits.

ANOTHER.
> Aye, that were next in my desire
>> To Athens, where good spirits dwell....

ANOTHER.
> Or Aetna's breast, the deeps of fire
>> That front the Tyrian's Citadel:
> First mother, she, of Sicily
>> And mighty mountains: fame hath told
>> Their crowns of goodness manifold....

ANOTHER.
> And, close beyond the narrowing sea,
> A sister land, where float enchanted
>> Ionian summits, wave on wave,
> And Crathis of the burning tresses
> Makes red the happy vale, and blesses
> With gold of fountains spirit-haunted
>> Homes of true men and brave!

LEADER.
> But lo, who cometh: and his lips
>> Grave with the weight of dooms unknown:
> A Herald from the Grecian ships.
>> Swift comes he, hot-foot to be done
> And finished. Ah, what bringeth he
> Of news or judgment? Slaves are we,
>> Spoils that the Greek hath won!

[TALTHYBIUS [14], followed by some Soldiers, enters from the left.]

TALTHYBIUS.
> Thou know'st me, Hecuba. Often have I crossed
> Thy plain with tidings from the Hellene host.
> 'Tis I, Talthybius.... Nay, of ancient use
> Thou know'st me. And I come to bear thee news.

HECUBA.
>> Ah me, 'tis here, 'tis here,
> Women of Troy, our long embosomed fear!

TALTHYBIUS.
>The lots are cast, if that it was ye feared.

HECUBA.
>What lord, what land.... Ah me,
>Phthia or Thebes, or sea-worn Thessaly?

TALTHYBIUS.
>Each hath her own. Ye go not in one herd.

HECUBA.
>Say then what lot hath any? What of joy
>Falls, or can fall on any child of Troy?

TALTHYBIUS.
>I know: but make thy questions severally.

HECUBA.
>My stricken one must be
>Still first. Say how Cassandra's portion lies.

TALTHYBIUS.
>Chosen from all for Agamemnon's prize!

HECUBA.
>How, for his Spartan bride
>A tirewoman? For Helen's sister's pride?

TALTHYBIUS.
>Nay, nay: a bride herself, for the King's bed.

HECUBA.
>The sainted of Apollo? And her own
>Prize that God promised
>Out of the golden clouds, her virgin crown?...

TALTHYBIUS.
>He loved her for that same strange holiness.

HECUBA.
>Daughter, away, away,
>Cast all away,
>The haunted Keys [15], the lonely stole's array
>That kept thy body like a sacred place!

TALTHYBIUS.
>Is't not rare fortune that the King hath smiled
>On such a maid?

HECUBA.
>What of that other child
>Ye reft from me but now?

TALTHYBIUS (speaking with some constraint).
>Polyxena? Or what child meanest thou?

HECUBA.
>The same. What man now hath her, or what doom?

TALTHYBIUS.
>She rests apart, to watch Achilles' tomb.

HECUBA.
>To watch a tomb? My daughter? What is this?...
>Speak, Friend? What fashion of the laws of Greece?

TALTHYBIUS.
>Count thy maid happy! She hath naught of ill
>To fear....

HECUBA.
>What meanest thou? She liveth still?

TALTHYBIUS.
>I mean, she hath one toil [16] that holds her free
>From all toil else.

HECUBA.
>   What of Andromache,
>   Wife of mine iron-hearted Hector, where
>   Journeyeth she?

TALTHYBIUS.
>   Pyrrhus, Achilles' son, hath taken her.

HECUBA.
>   And I, whose slave am I,
>   The shaken head, the arm that creepeth by,
>   Staff-crutchèd, like to fall?

TALTHYBIUS.
>   Odysseus [17], Ithaca's king, hath thee for thrall.

HECUBA.
>   Beat, beat the crownless head:
>   Rend the cheek till the tears run red!
>   A lying man and a pitiless
>   Shall be lord of me, a heart full-flown
>   With scorn of righteousness:
>   O heart of a beast where law is none,
>   Where all things change so that lust be fed,
>   The oath and the deed, the right and the wrong,
>   Even the hate of the forked tongue:
>   Even the hate turns and is cold,
>   False as the love that was false of old!
>
>   O Women of Troy, weep for me!
>   Yea, I am gone: I am gone my ways.
>   Mine is the crown of misery,
>   The bitterest day of all our days.

LEADER.
>   Thy fate thou knowest, Queen: but I know not
>   What lord of South or North has won my lot.

TALTHYBIUS.
Go, seek Cassandra, men! Make your best speed,
That I may leave her with the King, and lead
These others to their divers lords.... Ha, there!
What means that sudden light? Is it the flare
Of torches?

[Light is seen shining through the crevices of the second hut on the
right. He moves towards it.]

Would they fire their prison rooms,
Or how, these dames of Troy?—'Fore God, the dooms
Are known, and now they burn themselves and die [18]
Rather than sail with us! How savagely
In days like these a free neck chafes beneath
Its burden!... Open! Open quick! Such death
Were bliss to them, it may be: but 'twill bring
Much wrath, and leave me shamed before the King!

HECUBA.
There is no fire, no peril: 'tis my child,
Cassandra, by the breath of God made wild.

[The door opens from within and CASSANDRA enters, white-robed
and wreathed like a Priestess, a great torch in her hand. She is
singing softly to herself and does not see the Herald or the scene
before her.]

CASSANDRA.
Lift, lift it high: [Strophe.]
Give it to mine hand!
Lo, I bear a flame
Unto God! I praise his name.
I light with a burning brand
This sanctuary.
Blessèd is he that shall wed,
And blessèd, blessèd am I
In Argos: a bride to lie
With a king in a king's bed.

Hail, O Hymen [19] red,
O Torch that makest one!
Weepest thou, Mother mine own?
Surely thy cheek is pale
With tears, tears that wail
For a land and a father dead.
But I go garlanded:
I am the Bride of Desire:
Therefore my torch is borne—
Lo, the lifting of morn,
Lo, the leaping of fire!—

For thee, O Hymen bright,
For thee, O Moon of the Deep,
So Law hath charged, for the light
Of a maid's last sleep.

Awake, O my feet, awake: [Antistrophe.]
Our father's hope is won!
Dance as the dancing skies
Over him, where he lies
Happy beneath the sun!...
Lo, the Ring that I make....

[She makes a circle round her with a torch, and visions appear to her.]

Apollo!... Ah, is it thou?
O shrine in the laurels cold,
I bear thee still, as of old,
Mine incense! Be near to me now.

[She waves the torch as though bearing incense.]

O Hymen, Hymen fleet:
Quick torch that makest one!...
How? Am I still alone?
Laugh as I laugh, and twine
In the dance, O Mother mine:
Dear feet, be near my feet!

Come, greet ye Hymen, greet
   Hymen with songs of pride:
Sing to him loud and long,
Cry, cry, when the song
   Faileth, for joy of the bride!

O Damsels girt in the gold
   Of Ilion, cry, cry ye,
For him that is doomed of old
   To be lord of me!

LEADER.
   O hold the damsel, lest her trancèd feet
   Lift her afar, Queen, toward the Hellene fleet!

HECUBA.
   O Fire, Fire, where men make marriages
   Surely thou hast thy lot; but what are these
   Thou bringest flashing? Torches savage-wild
   And far from mine old dreams.—Alas, my child,
   How little dreamed I then of wars or red
   Spears of the Greek to lay thy bridal bed!
   Give me thy brand; it hath no holy blaze
   Thus in thy frenzy flung. Nor all thy days
   Nor all thy griefs have changed them yet, nor learned
   Wisdom.—Ye women, bear the pine half burned
   To the chamber back; and let your drownèd eyes
   Answer the music of these bridal cries!

[She takes the torch and gives it to one of the women.]

CASSANDRA.
   O Mother, fill mine hair with happy flowers,
   And speed me forth. Yea, if my spirit cowers,
   Drive me with wrath! So liveth Loxias [20],
   A bloodier bride than ever Helen was
   Go I to Agamemnon, Lord most high
   Of Hellas!... I shall kill him, mother; I
   Shall kill him, and lay waste his house with fire
   As he laid ours. My brethren and my sire
   Shall win again.... [21]

(Checking herself) But part I must let be,
And speak not. Not the axe that craveth me,
And more than me; not the dark wanderings
Of mother-murder that my bridal brings,
And all the House of Atreus down, down, down....

   Nay, I will show thee. Even now this town
Is happier than the Greeks. I know the power
Of God is on me: but this little hour,
Wilt thou but listen, I will hold him back!
   One love, one woman's beauty, o'er the track
Of hunted Helen, made their myriads fall.
And this their King so wise [22], who ruleth all,
What wrought he? Cast out Love that Hate might feed:
Gave to his brother his own child, his seed
Of gladness, that a woman fled, and fain
To fly for ever, should be turned again!
   So the days waned, and armies on the shore
Of Simois stood and strove and died. Wherefore?
No man had moved their landmarks; none had shook
Their wallèd towns.—And they whom Ares took,
Had never seen their children: no wife came
With gentle arms to shroud the limbs of them
For burial, in a strange and angry earth
Laid dead. And there at home, the same long dearth:
Women that lonely died, and aged men
Waiting for sons that ne'er should turn again,
Nor know their graves, nor pour drink-offerings,
To still the unslakèd dust. These be the things
The conquering Greek hath won!
                       But we—what pride,
What praise of men were sweeter?—fighting died
To save our people. And when war was red
Around us, friends upbore the gentle dead
Home, and dear women's heads about them wound
White shrouds, and here they sleep in the old ground
Belovèd. And the rest long days fought on,
Dwelling with wives and children, not alone
And joyless, like these Greeks.
                       And Hector's woe,
What is it? He is gone, and all men know

His glory, and how true a heart he bore.
It is the gift the Greek hath brought! Of yore
Men saw him not, nor knew him. Yea, and even
Paris [23] hath loved withal a child of heaven:
Else had his love but been as others are.

   Would ye be wise, ye Cities, fly from war!
Yet if war come, there is a crown in death
For her that striveth well and perisheth
Unstained: to die in evil were the stain!
Therefore, O Mother, pity not thy slain,
Nor Troy, nor me, the bride. Thy direst foe
And mine by this my wooing is brought low.

TALTHYBIUS (at last breaking through the spell that has held him).
   I swear, had not Apollo made thee mad,
   Not lightly hadst thou flung this shower of bad
   Bodings, to speed my General o'er the seas!
      'Fore God, the wisdoms and the greatnesses
   Of seeming, are they hollow all, as things
   Of naught? This son of Atreus, of all kings
   Most mighty, hath so bowed him to the love
   Of this mad maid, and chooseth her above
   All women! By the Gods, rude though I be,
   I would not touch her hand!
                              Look thou; I see
   Thy lips are blind, and whatso words they speak,
   Praises of Troy or shamings of the Greek,
   I cast to the four winds! Walk at my side
   In peace!... And heaven content him of his bride!

[He moves as though to go, but turns to HECUBA, and speaks more
   gently.]

   And thou shalt follow to Odysseus' host
   When the word comes. 'Tis a wise queen [24] thou go'st
   To serve, and gentle: so the Ithacans say.

CASSANDRA (seeing for the first time the Herald and all the scene).
    How fierce a slave!... O Heralds, Heralds!
        Yea,
    Voices of Death [25]; and mists are over them
    Of dead men's anguish, like a diadem,
    These weak abhorred things that serve the hate
    Of kings and peoples!...
                    To Odysseus' gate
    My mother goeth, say'st thou? Is God's word
    As naught, to me in silence ministered,
    That in this place she dies? [26]... (To herself) No more; no more!
    Why should I speak the shame of them, before
    They come?... Little he knows, that hard-beset
    Spirit, what deeps of woe await him yet;
    Till all these tears of ours and harrowings
    Of Troy, by his, shall be as golden things.
    Ten years behind ten years athwart his way
    Waiting: and home, lost and unfriended....
                        Nay:
    Why should Odysseus' labours vex my breath?
    On; hasten; guide me to the house of Death,
    To lie beside my bridegroom!...
                    Thou Greek King,
    Who deem'st thy fortune now so high a thing,
    Thou dust of the earth, a lowlier bed I see,
    In darkness, not in light, awaiting thee:
    And with thee, with thee ... there, where yawneth plain
    A rift of the hills, raging with winter rain,
    Dead ... and out-cast ... and naked.... It is I
    Beside my bridegroom: and the wild beasts cry,
    And ravin on God's chosen!

[She clasps her hands to her brow and feels the wreaths.]

O, ye wreaths!
Ye garlands of my God, whose love yet breathes
About me, shapes of joyance mystical,
Begone! I have forgot the festival,
Forgot the joy. Begone! I tear ye, so,
From off me!... Out on the swift winds they go.
With flesh still clean I give them back to thee,
Still white, O God, O light that leadest me!

[Turning upon the Herald.]

Where lies the galley? Whither shall I tread?
See that your watch be set, your sail be spread
The wind comes quick [27]! Three Powers—mark me, thou!—
There be in Hell, and one walks with thee now!
    Mother, farewell, and weep not! O my sweet
City, my earth-clad brethren, and thou great
Sire that begat us, but a space, ye Dead,
And I am with you, yea, with crowned head
I come, and shining from the fires that feed
On these that slay us now, and all their seed!

[She goes out, followed by Talthybius and the Soldiers Hecuba, after
    waiting for an instant motionless, falls to the ground.]

LEADER OF CHORUS.
    The Queen, ye Watchers! See, she falls, she falls,
    Rigid without a word! O sorry thralls,
    Too late! And will ye leave her downstricken,
    A woman, and so old? Raise her again!

[Some women go to HECUBA, but she refuses their aid and speaks
    without rising.]

HECUBA.
    Let lie ... the love we seek not is no love....
    This ruined body! Is the fall thereof
    Too deep for all that now is over me
    Of anguish, and hath been, and yet shall be?
    Ye Gods.... Alas! Why call on things so weak
    For aid? Yet there is something that doth seek,

Crying, for God, when one of us hath woe.
O, I will think of things gone long ago
And weave them to a song, like one more tear
In the heart of misery.... All kings we were;
And I must wed a king. And sons I brought
My lord King, many sons ... nay, that were naught;
But high strong princes, of all Troy the best.
Hellas nor Troäs nor the garnered East
Held such a mother! And all these things beneath
The Argive spear I saw cast down in death,
And shore these tresses at the dead men's feet.

    Yea, and the gardener of my garden great,
It was not any noise of him nor tale
I wept for; these eyes saw him, when the pale
Was broke, and there at the altar Priam fell
Murdered, and round him all his citadel
Sacked. And my daughters, virgins of the fold,
Meet to be brides of mighty kings, behold,
'Twas for the Greek I bred them! All are gone;
And no hope left, that I shall look upon
Their faces any more, nor they on mine.

    And now my feet tread on the utmost line:
An old, old slave-woman, I pass below
Mine enemies' gates; and whatso task they know
For this age basest, shall be mine; the door,
Bowing, to shut and open.... I that bore
Hector!... and meal to grind, and this racked head
Bend to the stones after a royal bed;
Tom rags about me, aye, and under them
Tom flesh; 'twill make a woman sick for shame!
Woe's me; and all that one man's arms might hold
One woman, what long seas have o'er me rolled
And roll for ever!... O my child, whose white
Soul laughed amid the laughter of God's light,
Cassandra, what hands and how strange a day
Have loosed thy zone! And thou, Polyxena,
Where art thou? And my sons? Not any seed
Of man nor woman now shall help my need.

    Why raise me any more? What hope have I
To hold me? Take this slave that once trod high
In Ilion; cast her on her bed of clay
Rock-pillowed, to lie down, and pass away

Wasted with tears. And whatso man they call
Happy, believe not ere the last day fall!

* * * * *

CHORUS [28]. [Strophe.]
 O Muse, be near me now, and make
 A strange song for Ilion's sake,
Till a tone of tears be about mine ears
 And out of my lips a music break
 For Troy, Troy, and the end of the years:
  When the wheels of the Greek above me pressed,
  And the mighty horse-hoofs beat my breast;
 And all around were the Argive spears
 A towering Steed of golden rein—
  O gold without, dark steel within!—
 Ramped in our gates; and all the plain
  Lay silent where the Greeks had been.
 And a cry broke from all the folk
 Gathered above on Ilion's rock:
 "Up, up, O fear is over now!
  To Pallas, who hath saved us living,
 To Pallas bear this victory-vow!"
 Then rose the old man from his room,
 The merry damsel left her loom,
 And each bound death about his brow
  With minstrelsy and high thanksgiving!

[Antistrophe.]

 O, swift were all in Troy that day,
 And girt them to the portal-way,
Marvelling at that mountain Thing
 Smooth-carven, where the Argives lay,
 And wrath, and Ilion's vanquishing:
  Meet gift for her that spareth not [29],
  Heaven's yokeless Rider. Up they brought
 Through the steep gates her offering:
 Like some dark ship that climbs the shore
  On straining cables, up, where stood
 Her marble throne, her hallowed floor,
  Who lusted for her people's blood.

A very weariness of joy
Fell with the evening over Troy:
And lutes of Afric mingled there
    With Phrygian songs: and many a maiden,
With white feet glancing light as air,
Made happy music through the gloom:
And fires on many an inward room
All night broad-flashing, flung their glare
    On laughing eyes and slumber-laden.

A MAIDEN.

I was among the dancers there
    To Artemis [30], and glorying sang
Her of the Hills, the Maid most fair,
    Daughter of Zeus: and, lo, there rang
A shout out of the dark, and fell
    Deathlike from street to street, and made
A silence in the citadel:
    And a child cried, as if afraid,
And hid him in his mother's veil.
    Then stalked the Slayer from his den,
The hand of Pallas served her well!
    O blood, blood of Troy was deep
    About the streets and altars then:
And in the wedded rooms of sleep,
    Lo, the desolate dark alone,
    And headless things, men stumbled on.

And forth, lo, the women go,
The crown of War, the crown of Woe,
To bear the children of the foe
    And weep, weep, for Ilion!

* * * * *

[As the song ceases a chariot is seen approaching from the town, laden with spoils. On it sits a mourning Woman with a child in her arms.]

LEADER.
Lo, yonder on the heapèd crest
Of a Greek wain, Andromachê [31],
As one that o'er an unknown sea
Tosseth; and on her wave-borne breast
Her loved one clingeth, Hector's child,
Astyanax.... O most forlorn
Of women, whither go'st thou, borne
'Mid Hector's bronzen arms, and piled
Spoils of the dead, and pageantry
Of them that hunted Ilion down?
Aye, richly thy new lord shall crown
The mountain shrines of Thessaly!

ANDROMACHE

[Strophe I.]

Forth to the Greek I go,
Driven as a beast is driven.

HEC. Woe, woe!

AND. Nay, mine is woe:
Woe to none other given,
And the song and the crown therefor!

HEC. O Zeus!

AND. He hates thee sore!

HEC. Children!

AND. No more, no more
To aid thee: their strife is striven!

HECUBA.

[Antistrophe I.]

Troy, Troy is gone!

AND. Yea, and her treasure parted.

HEC. Gone, gone, mine own
      Children, the noble-hearted!

AND. Sing sorrow....

HEC. For me, for me!

AND. Sing for the Great City,
      That falleth, falleth to be
        A shadow, a fire departed.

ANDROMACHE.

[Strophe 2.]

    Come to me, O my lover!

HEC. The dark shroudeth him over,
      My flesh, woman, not thine, not thine!

AND. Make of thine arms my cover!

HECUBA.

[Antistrophe 2.]

    O thou whose wound was deepest,
    Thou that my children keepest,
    Priam, Priam, O age-worn King,
      Gather me where thou sleepest.

ANDROMACHE (her hands upon her heart).

[Strophe 3.]

    O here is the deep of desire,

HEC. (How? And is this not woe?)

AND. For a city burned with fire;

HEC. (It beateth, blow on blow.)

AND. God's wrath for Paris, thy son, that he died not long ago:

> Who sold for his evil love
> Troy and the towers thereof:
> Therefore the dead men lie
> Naked, beneath the eye
> Of Pallas, and vultures croak
>   And flap for joy:
> So Love hath laid his yoke
>   On the neck of Troy!

HECUBA.

[Antistrophe 3.]

> O mine own land, my home,

AND. (I weep for thee, left forlorn,)

HEC. See'st thou what end is come?

AND. (And the house where my babes were born.)

HEC. A desolate Mother we leave, O children, a City of scorn:

> Even as the sound of a song [32]
> Left by the way, but long
> Remembered, a tune of tears
> Falling where no man hears,
> In the old house, as rain,
>   For things loved of yore:
> But the dead hath lost his pain
>   And weeps no more.

LEADER.
> How sweet are tears to them in bitter stress,
> And sorrow, and all the songs of heaviness.

ANDROMACHE [33].
> Mother of him of old, whose mighty spear
> Smote Greeks like chaff, see'st thou what things are here?

HECUBA.

    I see God's hand, that buildeth a great crown
    For littleness, and hath cast the mighty down.

ANDROMACHE.

    I and my babe are driven among the droves
    Of plundered cattle. O, when fortune moves
    So swift, the high heart like a slave beats low.

HECUBA.

    'Tis fearful to be helpless. Men but now
    Have taken Cassandra, and I strove in vain.

ANDROMACHE.

    Ah, woe is me; hath Ajax come again?
    But other evil yet is at thy gate.

HECUBA.

    Nay, Daughter, beyond number, beyond weight
    My evils are! Doom raceth against doom.

ANDROMACHE.

    Polyxena across Achilles' tomb
    Lies slain, a gift flung to the dreamless dead.

HECUBA.

    My sorrow!... 'Tis but what Talthybius said:
    So plain a riddle, and I read it not.

ANDROMACHE.

    I saw her lie, and stayed this chariot;
    And raiment wrapt on her dead limbs, and beat
    My breast for her.

HECUBA (to herself).

                      O the foul sin of it!
    The wickedness! My child. My child! Again
    I cry to thee. How cruelly art thou slain!

ANDROMACHE.
  She hath died her death, and howso dark it be,
  Her death is sweeter than my misery.

HECUBA.
  Death cannot be what Life is, Child; the cup
  Of Death is empty, and Life hath always hope.

ANDROMACHE.
  O Mother, having ears, hear thou this word
  Fear-conquering, till thy heart as mine be stirred
  With joy. To die is only not to be;
  And better to be dead than grievously
  Living. They have no pain, they ponder not
  Their own wrong. But the living that is brought
  From joy to heaviness, his soul doth roam,
  As in a desert, lost, from its old home.
  Thy daughter lieth now as one unborn,
  Dead, and naught knowing of the lust and scorn
  That slew her. And I ... long since I drew my bow
  Straight at the heart of good fame; and I know
  My shaft hit; and for that am I the more
  Fallen from peace. All that men praise us for,
  I loved for Hector's sake, and sought to win.
  I knew that alway, be there hurt therein
  Or utter innocence, to roam abroad
  Hath ill report for women; so I trod
  Down the desire thereof, and walked my way
  In mine own garden. And light words and gay
  Parley of women never passed my door.
  The thoughts of mine own heart ... I craved no more....
  Spoke with me, and I was happy. Constantly
  I brought fair silence and a tranquil eye
  For Hector's greeting, and watched well the way
  Of living, where to guide and where obey.
    And, lo! some rumour of this peace, being gone
  Forth to the Greek, hath cursed me. Achilles' son,
  So soon as I was taken, for his thrall
  Chose me. I shall do service in the hall
  Of them that slew.... How? Shall I thrust aside
  Hector's beloved face, and open wide

My heart to this new lord? Oh, I should stand
A traitor to the dead! And if my hand
And flesh shrink from him ... lo, wrath and despite
O'er all the house, and I a slave!
                                    One night,
One night ... aye, men have said it ... maketh tame
A woman in a man's arms.... O shame, shame!
What woman's lips can so forswear her dead,
And give strange kisses in another's bed?
Why, not a dumb beast, not a colt will run
In the yoke untroubled, when her mate is gone—
A thing not in God's image, dull, unmoved
Of reason. O my Hector! best beloved,
That, being mine, wast all in all to me,
My prince, my wise one, O my majesty
Of valiance! No man's touch had ever come
Near me, when thou from out my father's home
Didst lead me and make me thine.... And thou art dead,
And I war-flung to slavery and the bread
Of shame in Hellas, over bitter seas!
    What knoweth she of evils like to these,
That dead Polyxena, thou weepest for?
There liveth not in my life any more
The hope that others have. Nor will I tell
The lie to mine own heart, that aught is well
Or shall be well.... Yet, O, to dream were sweet!

LEADER.

Thy feet have trod the pathway of my feet,
And thy clear sorrow teacheth me mine own.

HECUBA.

Lo, yonder ships: I ne'er set foot on one,
But tales and pictures tell, when over them
Breaketh a storm not all too strong to stem,
Each man strives hard, the tiller gripped, the mast
Manned, the hull baled, to face it: till at last
Too strong breaks the o'erwhelming sea: lo, then
They cease, and yield them up as broken men
To fate and the wild waters. Even so
I in my many sorrows bear me low,
Nor curse, nor strive that other things may be.

The great wave rolled from God hath conquered me.
   But, O, let Hector and the fates that fell
On Hector, sleep. Weep for him ne'er so well,
Thy weeping shall not wake him. Honour thou
The new lord that is set above thee now,
And make of thine own gentle piety
A prize to lure his heart. So shalt thou be
A strength to them that love us, and—God knows,
It may be—rear this babe among his foes,
My Hector's child, to manhood and great aid
For Ilion. So her stones may yet be laid
One on another, if God will, and wrought
Again to a city! Ah, how thought to thought
Still beckons!... But what minion of the Greek
Is this that cometh, with new words to speak?

[Enter TALTHYBIUS with a band of Soldiers. He comes forward slowly and with evident disquiet.]

TALTHYBIUS.
   Spouse of the noblest heart that beat in Troy,
Andromache, hate me not! 'Tis not in joy
I tell thee. But the people and the Kings
Have with one voice....

ANDROMACHE.
                What is it? Evil things
Are on thy lips!

TALTHYBIUS.
                'Tis ordered, this child.... Oh,
How can I tell her of it?

ANDROMACHE.
                Doth he not go
With me, to the same master?

TALTHYBIUS.
                There is none
In Greece, shall e'er be master of thy son.

ANDROMACHE.

How? Will they leave him here to build again
The wreck?...

TALTHYBIUS.

I know not how to tell thee plain!

ANDROMACHE.

Thou hast a gentle heart ... if it be ill,
And not good, news thou hidest!

TALTHYBIUS.

'Tis their will
Thy son shall die.... The whole vile thing is said
Now!

ANDROMACHE.

Oh, I could have borne mine enemy's bed!

TALTHYBIUS.

And speaking in the council of the host
Odysseus hath prevailed—

ANDROMACHE.

O lost! lost! lost!...
Forgive me! It is not easy....

TALTHYBIUS.

... That the son
Of one so perilous be not fostered on
To manhood—

ANDROMACHE.

God; may his own counsel fall
On his own sons!

TALTHYBIUS.
               ... But from this crested wall
Of Troy be dashed, and die.... Nay, let the thing
Be done. Thou shalt be wiser so. Nor cling
So fiercely to him. Suffer as a brave
Woman in bitter pain; nor think to have
Strength which thou hast not. Look about thee here!
Canst thou see help, or refuge anywhere?
Thy land is fallen and thy lord, and thou
A prisoner and alone, one woman; how
Canst battle against us? For thine own good
I would not have thee strive, nor make ill blood
And shame about thee.... Ah, nor move thy lips
In silence there, to cast upon the ships
Thy curse! One word of evil to the host,
This babe shall have no burial, but be tossed
Naked.... Ah, peace! And bear as best thou may,
War's fortune. So thou shalt not go thy way
Leaving this child unburied; nor the Greek
Be stern against thee, if thy heart be meek!

ANDROMACHE (to the child).
    Go, die, my best-beloved, my cherished one,
In fierce men's hands, leaving me here alone.
Thy father was too valiant; that is why
They slay thee! Other children, like to die,
Might have been spared for that. But on thy head
His good is turned to evil.
                    O thou bed
And bridal; O the joining of the hand,
That led me long ago to Hector's land
To bear, O not a lamb for Grecian swords
To slaughter, but a Prince o'er all the hordes
Enthroned of wide-flung Asia.... Weepest thou?
Nay, why, my little one? Thou canst not know.
And Father will not come; he will not come;
Not once, the great spear flashing, and the tomb
Riven to set thee free! Not one of all
His brethren, nor the might of Ilion's wall.
    How shall it be? One horrible spring ... deep, deep
Down. And thy neck.... Ah God, so cometh sleep!...

And none to pity thee!... Thou little thing
That curlest in my arms, what sweet scents cling
All round thy neck! Belovèd; can it be
All nothing, that this bosom cradled thee
And fostered; all the weary nights, wherethrough
I watched upon thy sickness, till I grew
Wasted with watching? Kiss me. This one time;
Not ever again. Put up thine arms, and climb
About my neck: now, kiss me, lips to lips....

   O, ye have found an anguish that outstrips
All tortures of the East, ye gentle Greeks!
Why will ye slay this innocent, that seeks
No wrong?... O Helen, Helen, thou ill tree
That Tyndareus planted, who shall deem of thee
As child of Zeus? O, thou hast drawn thy breath
From many fathers, Madness, Hate, red Death,
And every rotting poison of the sky!
Zeus knows thee not, thou vampire, draining dry.
Greece and the world! God hate thee and destroy,
That with those beautiful eyes hast blasted Troy,
And made the far-famed plains a waste withal.

   Quick! take him: drag him: cast him from the wall,
If cast ye will! Tear him, ye beasts, be swift!
God hath undone me, and I cannot lift
One hand, one hand, to save my child from death....
O, hide my head for shame: fling me beneath
Your galleys' benches!...

[She swoons: then half-rising.]

                Quick: I must begone
To the bridal.... I have lost my child, my own!

[The Soldiers close round her.]

LEADER.

   O Troy ill-starred; for one strange woman, one
Abhorrèd kiss, how are thine hosts undone!

TALTHYBIUS (bending over ANDROMACHE and gradually taking
the Child from her).

Come, Child: let be that clasp of love
   Outwearied! Walk thy ways with me,
Up to the crested tower, above
   Thy father's wall.... Where they decree
Thy soul shall perish.—Hold him: hold!—
   Would God some other man might ply
These charges, one of duller mould,
   And nearer to the iron than I!

HECUBA.

O Child, they rob us of our own,
   Child of my Mighty One outworn:
Ours, ours thou art!—Can aught be done
   Of deeds, can aught of pain be borne,
To aid thee?—Lo, this beaten head,
This bleeding bosom! These I spread
As gifts to thee. I can thus much.
   Woe, woe for Troy, and woe for thee!
What fall yet lacketh, ere we touch
   The last dead deep of misery?

[The Child, who has started back from TALTHYBIUS, is taken up by
one of the Soldiers and borne back towards the city, while
ANDROMACHE is set again on the Chariot and driven off
towards the ships. TALTHYBIUS goes with the Child.]

* * * * *

CHORUS.

[Strophe I.]

In Salamis, filled with the foaming [34]
   Of billows and murmur of bees,
Old Telamon stayed from his roaming,
   Long ago, on a throne of the seas;
Looking out on the hills olive-laden,
   Enchanted, where first from the earth
The grey-gleaming fruit of the Maiden
      Athena had birth;
A soft grey crown for a city

Belovèd a City of Light:
Yet he rested not there, nor had pity,
   But went forth in his might,
Where Heracles wandered, the lonely
  Bow-bearer, and lent him his hands
For the wrecking of one land only,
Of Ilion, Ilion only,
   Most hated of lands!

[Antistrophe I.]

Of the bravest of Hellas he made him
  A ship-folk, in wrath for the Steeds,
And sailed the wide waters, and stayed him
  At last amid Simoïs' reeds;
And the oars beat slow in the river,
  And the long ropes held in the strand,
And he felt for his bow and his quiver,
   The wrath of his hand.
And the old king died; and the towers
  That Phoebus had builded did fall,
And his wrath, as a flame that devours,
   Ran red over all;
And the fields and the woodlands lay blasted,
  Long ago. Yea, twice hath the Sire
Uplifted his hand and downcast it
On the wall of the Dardan, downcast it
   As a sword and as fire.

[Strophe 2.]

In vain, all in vain,
  O thou 'mid the wine-jars golden
   That movest in delicate joy,
   Ganymêdês, child of Troy,
The lips of the Highest drain
  The cup in thine hand upholden:
And thy mother, thy mother that bore thee,
  Is wasted with fire and torn;
   And the voice of her shores is heard,
   Wild, as the voice of a bird,
For lovers and children before thee
  Crying, and mothers outworn.
And the pools of thy bathing [35] are perished,
  And the wind-strewn ways of thy feet:
Yet thy face as aforetime is cherished

Of Zeus, and the breath of it sweet;
Yea, the beauty of Calm is upon it
   In houses at rest and afar.
But thy land, He hath wrecked and o'erthrown it
      In the wailing of war.

                              [Antistrophe 2.]

O Love, ancient Love,
   Of old to the Dardan given;
      Love of the Lords of the Sky;
      How didst thou lift us high
In Ilion, yea, and above
   All cities, as wed with heaven!
For Zeus—O leave it unspoken:
   But alas for the love of the Morn;
      Morn of the milk-white wing,
      The gentle, the earth-loving,
That shineth on battlements broken
   In Troy, and a people forlorn!
And, lo, in her bowers Tithônus,
   Our brother, yet sleeps as of old:
O, she too hath loved us and known us,
   And the Steeds of her star, flashing gold,
Stooped hither and bore him above us;
   Then blessed we the Gods in our joy.
But all that made them to love us
      Hath perished from Troy.

                    * * * * *

[As the song ceases, the King MENELAUS enters, richly armed and
   followed by a bodyguard of Soldiers. He is a prey to violent and
   conflicting emotions.]

MENELAUS [36].
   How bright the face of heaven, and how sweet
   The air this day, that layeth at my feet
   The woman that I.... Nay: 'twas not for her
   I came. 'Twas for the man, the cozener
   And thief, that ate with me and stole away
   My bride. But Paris lieth, this long day,
   By God's grace, under the horse-hoofs of the Greek,
   And round him all his land. And now I seek....

Curse her! I scarce can speak the name she bears,
That was my wife. Here with the prisoners
They keep her, in these huts, among the hordes
Of numbered slaves.—The host whose labouring swords
Won her, have given her up to me, to fill
My pleasure; perchance kill her, or not kill,
But lead her home.—Methinks I have foregone
The slaying of Helen here in Ilion....
Over the long seas I will bear her back,
And there, there, cast her out to whatso wrack
Of angry death they may devise, who know
Their dearest dead for her in Ilion.—Ho!
Ye soldiers! Up into the chambers where
She croucheth! Grip the long blood-reeking hair,
And drag her to mine eyes ... [Controlling himself.]
                                        And when there come
Fair breezes, my long ships shall bear her home.

[The Soldiers go to force open the door of the second hut on the left.]

HECUBA.

Thou deep Base of the World [37], and thou high Throne
Above the World, whoe'er thou art, unknown
And hard of surmise, Chain of Things that be,
Or Reason of our Reason; God, to thee
I lift my praise, seeing the silent road
That bringeth justice ere the end be trod
To all that breathes and dies.

MENELAUS (turning).

                                        Ha! who is there
That prayeth heaven, and in so strange a prayer?

HECUBA.

I bless thee, Menelaus, I bless thee,
If thou wilt slay her! Only fear to see
Her visage, lest she snare thee and thou fall!
She snareth strong men's eyes; she snareth tall
Cities; and fire from out her eateth up
Houses. Such magic hath she, as a cup
Of death!... Do I not know her? Yea, and thou,
And these that lie around, do they not know?

[The Soldiers return from the hut and stand aside to let HELEN pass
    between them. She comes through them, gentle and unafraid; there
    is no disorder in her raiment.]

HELEN.

King Menelaus, thy first deed might make
A woman fear. Into my chamber brake
Thine armèd men, and lead me wrathfully.
    Methinks, almost, I know thou hatest me.
Yet I would ask thee, what decree is gone
Forth for my life or death?

MENELAUS (struggling with his emotion).

                                There was not one
That scrupled for thee. All, all with one will
Gave thee to me, whom thou hast wronged, to kill!

HELEN.

And is it granted that I speak, or no,
In answer to them ere I die, to show
I die most wronged and innocent?

MENELAUS.

                                I seek
To kill thee, woman; not to hear thee speak!

HECUBA.

O hear her! She must never die unheard,
King Menelaus! And give me the word
To speak in answer! All the wrong she wrought
Away from thee, in Troy, thou knowest not.
The whole tale set together is a death
Too sure; she shall not 'scape thee!

MENELAUS.

                                'Tis but breath
And time. For thy sake, Hecuba, if she need
To speak, I grant the prayer. I have no heed
Nor mercy—let her know it well—for her!

HELEN.

> It may be that, how false or true soe'er
> Thou deem me, I shall win no word from thee.
> So sore thou holdest me thine enemy.
> Yet I will take what words I think thy heart
> Holdeth of anger: and in even part
> Set my wrong and thy wrong, and all that fell.

[Pointing to HECUBA.]

> She cometh first, who bare the seed and well
> Of springing sorrow, when to life she brought
> Paris: and that old King, who quenched not
> Quick in the spark, ere yet he woke to slay,
> The fire-brand's image [38].—But enough: a day
> Came, and this Paris judged beneath the trees
> Three Crowns of Life [39], three diverse Goddesses.
> The gift of Pallas was of War, to lead
> His East in conquering battles, and make bleed
> The hearths of Hellas. Hera held a Throne—
> If majesties he craved—to reign alone
> From Phrygia to the last realm of the West.
> And Cypris, if he deemed her loveliest,
> Beyond all heaven, made dreams about my face
> And for her grace gave me. And, lo! her grace
> Was judged the fairest, and she stood above
> Those twain.—Thus was I loved, and thus my love
> Hath holpen Hellas. No fierce Eastern crown
> Is o'er your lands, no spear hath cast them down.
> O, it was well for Hellas! But for me
> Most ill; caught up and sold across the sea
> For this my beauty; yea, dishonourèd
> For that which else had been about my head
> A crown of honour.... Ah, I see thy thought;
> The first plain deed, 'tis that I answer not,
> How in the dark out of thy house I fled....
> There came the Seed of Fire, this woman's seed;
> Came—O, a Goddess great walked with him then—
> This Alexander, Breaker-down-of-Men,
> This Paris [40], Strength-is-with-him; whom thou, whom—
> O false and light of heart—thou in thy room

Didst leave, and spreadest sail for Cretan seas,
Far, far from me!... And yet, how strange it is!
I ask not thee; I ask my own sad thought,
What was there in my heart, that I forgot
My home and land and all I loved, to fly
With a strange man? Surely it was not I,
But Cypris, there! Lay thou thy rod on her,
And be more high than Zeus and bitterer,
Who o'er all other spirits hath his throne,
But knows her chain must bind him. My wrong done
Hath its own pardon....

                    One word yet thou hast,
Methinks, of righteous seeming. When at last
The earth for Paris oped and all was o'er,
And her strange magic bound my feet no more,
Why kept I still his house, why fled not I
To the Argive ships?... Ah, how I strove to fly!
The old Gate-Warden [41] could have told thee all,
My husband, and the watchers from the wall;
It was not once they took me, with the rope
Tied, and this body swung in the air, to grope
Its way toward thee, from that dim battlement.

   Ah, husband still, how shall thy hand be bent
To slay me? Nay, if Right be come at last,
What shalt thou bring but comfort for pains past,
And harbour for a woman storm-driven:
A woman borne away by violent men:
And this one birthright of my beauty, this
That might have been my glory, lo, it is
A stamp that God hath burned, of slavery!

   Alas! and if thou cravest still to be
As one set above gods, inviolate,
'Tis but a fruitless longing holds thee yet.

LEADER.

   O Queen, think of thy children and thy land,
And break her spell! The sweet soft speech, the hand
And heart so fell: it maketh me afraid.

HECUBA.

Meseems her goddesses first cry mine aid
Against these lying lips!... Not Hera, nay,
Nor virgin Pallas deem I such low clay,
To barter their own folk, Argos and brave
Athens, to be trod down, the Phrygian's slave,
All for vain glory and a shepherd's prize
On Ida! Wherefore should great Hera's eyes
So hunger to be fair? She doth not use
To seek for other loves, being wed with Zeus.
And maiden Pallas ... did some strange god's face
Beguile her, that she craved for loveliness,
Who chose from God one virgin gift above
All gifts, and fleeth from the lips of love?

   Ah, deck not out thine own heart's evil springs
By making spirits of heaven as brutish things
And cruel. The wise may hear thee, and guess all!

   And Cypris must take ship-fantastical!
Sail with my son and enter at the gate
To seek thee! Had she willed it, she had sate
At peace in heaven, and wafted thee, and all
Amyclae with thee, under Ilion's wall.

   My son was passing beautiful, beyond
His peers; and thine own heart, that saw and conned
His face, became a spirit enchanting thee.
For all wild things that in mortality
Have being, are Aphroditê; and the name
She bears in heaven is born and writ of them.

   Thou sawest him in gold and orient vest
Shining, and lo, a fire about thy breast
Leapt! Thou hadst fed upon such little things,
Pacing thy ways in Argos. But now wings
Were come! Once free from Sparta, and there rolled
The Ilian glory, like broad streams of gold,
To steep thine arms and splash the towers! How small,
How cold that day was Menelaus' hall!

   Enough of that. It was by force my son
Took thee, thou sayst, and striving.... Yet not one
In Sparta knew! No cry, no sudden prayer
Rang from thy rooms that night.... Castor was there
To hear thee, and his brother: both true men,

Not yet among the stars! And after, when
Thou camest here to Troy, and in thy track
Argos and all its anguish and the rack
Of war—Ah God!—perchance men told thee 'Now
The Greek prevails in battle': then wouldst thou
Praise Menelaus, that my son might smart,
Striving with that old image in a heart
Uncertain still. Then Troy had victories:
And this Greek was as naught! Alway thine eyes
Watched Fortune's eyes, to follow hot where she
Led first. Thou wouldst not follow Honesty.

   Thy secret ropes, thy body swung to fall
Far, like a desperate prisoner, from the wall!
Who found thee so? When wast thou taken? Nay,
Hadst thou no surer rope, no sudden way
Of the sword, that any woman honest-souled
Had sought long since, loving her lord of old?

   Often and often did I charge thee; 'Go,
My daughter; go thy ways. My sons will know
New loves. I will give aid, and steal thee past
The Argive watch. O give us peace at last,
Us and our foes!' But out thy spirit cried
As at a bitter word. Thou hadst thy pride
In Alexander's house, and O, 'twas sweet
To hold proud Easterns bowing at thy feet.
They were great things to thee!... And comest thou now
Forth, and hast decked thy bosom and thy brow,
And breathest with thy lord the same blue air,
Thou evil heart? Low, low, with ravaged hair,
Rent raiment, and flesh shuddering, and within—
O shame at last, not glory for thy sin;
So face him if thou canst!... Lo, I have done.
Be true, O King; let Hellas bear her crown
Of Justice. Slay this woman, and upraise
The law for evermore: she that betrays
Her husband's bed, let her be judged and die.

LEADER.

   Be strong, O King; give judgment worthily
For thee and thy great house. Shake off thy long
Reproach; not weak, but iron against the wrong!

MENELAUS.

Thy thought doth walk with mine in one intent.
'Tis sure; her heart was willing, when she went
Forth to a stranger's bed. And all her fair
Tale of enchantment, 'tis a thing of air!...

[Turning furiously upon HELEN.]

Out, woman! There be those that seek thee yet
With stones! Go, meet them. So shall thy long debt
Be paid at last. And ere this night is o'er
Thy dead face shall dishonour me no more!

HELEN (kneeling before him and embracing him).

Behold, mine arms are wreathed about thy knees;
Lay not upon my head the phantasies
Of Heaven. Remember all, and slay me not!

HECUBA.

Remember them she murdered, them that fought
Beside thee, and their children! Hear that prayer!

MENELAUS.

Peace, agèd woman, peace! 'Tis not for her;
She is as naught to me.
        (To the Soldiers) ... March on before,
Ye ministers, and tend her to the shore ...
And have some chambered galley set for her,
Where she may sail the seas.

HECUBA.

                                If thou be there,
I charge thee, let not her set foot therein!

MENELAUS.

How? Shall the ship go heavier for her sin?

HECUBA.

A lover once, will alway love again.

MENELAUS.

If that he loved be evil, he will fain
Hate it!... Howbeit, thy pleasure shall be done.
Some other ship shall bear her, not mine own....
Thou counsellest very well.... And when we come
To Argos, then ... O then some pitiless doom
Well-earned, black as her heart! One that shall bind
Once for all time the law on womankind
Of faithfulness!... 'Twill be no easy thing,
God knoweth. But the thought thereof shall fling
A chill on the dreams of women, though they be
Wilder of wing and loathèd more than she!

[Exit, following HELEN, who is escorted by the Soldiers.]

* * * * *

CHORUS [42].

(Some Women.)

[Strophe I.]
And hast thou turned from the Altar of frankincense,
    And given to the Greek thy temple of Ilion?
The flame of the cakes of corn, is it gone from hence,
    The myrrh on the air and the wreathèd towers gone?
And Ida, dark Ida, where the wild ivy grows,
The glens that run as rivers from the summer-broken snows,
And the Rock, is it forgotten, where the first sunbeam glows,
    The lit house most holy of the Dawn?

(Others.)

[Antistrophe I.]
The sacrifice is gone and the sound of joy,
    The dancing under the stars and the night-long prayer:
The Golden Images and the Moons of Troy,
    The twelve Moons and the mighty names they bear:
My heart, my heart crieth, O Lord Zeus on high,
Were they all to thee as nothing, thou thronèd in the sky,
Thronèd in the fire-cloud, where a City, near to die,

Passeth in the wind and the flare?

(A Woman.)

[Strophe 2.]

Dear one, O husband mine,
    Thou in the dim dominions
Driftest with waterless lips,
Unburied; and me the ships
Shall bear o'er the bitter brine,
    Storm-birds upon angry pinions,
Where the towers of the Giants [43] shine
O'er Argos cloudily,
And the riders ride by the sea.

(Others.)

And children still in the Gate
    Crowd and cry,
A multitude desolate,
Voices that float and wait
    As the tears run dry:
'Mother, alone on the shore
    They drive me, far from thee:
Lo, the dip of the oar,
    The black hull on the sea!
Is it the Isle Immortal,
    Salamis, waits for me?
Is it the Rock that broods
Over the sundered floods
Of Corinth, the ancient portal
    Of Pelops' sovranty?'

(A Woman.)

[Antistrophe 2.]

Out in the waste of foam,
    Where rideth dark Menelaus,
Come to us there, O white
And jagged, with wild sea-light
And crashing of oar-blades, come,
    O thunder of God, and slay us:
While our tears are wet for home,

While out in the storm go we,
Slaves of our enemy!

(Others.)
And, God, may Helen be there [44],
    With mirror of gold,
Decking her face so fair,
Girl-like; and hear, and stare,
    And turn death-cold:
Never, ah, never more
    The hearth of her home to see,
Nor sand of the Spartan shore,
    Nor tombs where her fathers be,
Nor Athena's bronzen Dwelling,
    Nor the towers of Pitanê;
For her face was a dark desire
Upon Greece, and shame like fire,
And her dead are welling, welling,
    From red Simoïs to the sea!

* * * * *

[TALTHYBIUS, followed by one or two Soldiers and bearing the child
    ASTYANAX dead, is seen approaching.]

LEADER.
Ah, change on change! Yet each one racks
    This land with evil manifold;
    Unhappy wives of Troy, behold,
They bear the dead Astyanax,
Our prince, whom bitter Greeks this hour
Have hurled to death from Ilion's tower.

TALTHYBIUS.
One galley, Hecuba, there lingereth yet,
Lapping the wave, to gather the last freight
Of Pyrrhus' spoils for Thessaly. The chief
Himself long since hath parted, much in grief
For Pêleus' sake, his grandsire, whom, men say,
Acastus, Pelias' son, in war array
Hath driven to exile. Loath enough before
Was he to linger, and now goes the more

In haste, bearing Andromache, his prize.
'Tis she hath charmed these tears into mine eyes,
Weeping her fatherland, as o'er the wave
She gazed, and speaking words to Hector's grave.
Howbeit, she prayed us that due rites be done
For burial of this babe, thine Hector's son,
That now from Ilion's tower is fallen and dead.
And, lo! this great bronze-fronted shield, the dread
Of many a Greek, that Hector held in fray,
O never in God's name—so did she pray—
Be this borne forth to hang in Pêleus' hall
Or that dark bridal chamber, that the wall
May hurt her eyes; but here, in Troy o'erthrown,
Instead of cedar wood and vaulted stone,
Be this her child's last house.... And in thine hands
She bade me lay him, to be swathed in bands
Of death and garments, such as rest to thee
In these thy fallen fortunes; seeing that she
Hath gone her ways, and, for her master's haste,
May no more fold the babe unto his rest.
   Howbeit, so soon as he is garlanded
And robed, we will heap earth above his head
And lift our sails.... See all be swiftly done,
As thou art bidden. I have saved thee one
Labour. For as I passed Scamander's stream
Hard by, I let the waters run on him,
And cleansed his wounds.—See, I will go forth now
And break the hard earth for his grave: so thou
And I will haste together, to set free
Our oars at last to beat the homeward sea!

[He goes out with his Soldiers, leaving the body of the Child in
   HECUBA'S arms.]

HECUBA.

   Set the great orb of Hector's shield to lie
Here on the ground. 'Tis bitter that mine eye
Should see it.... O ye Argives, was your spear
Keen, and your hearts so low and cold, to fear
This babe? 'Twas a strange murder for brave men!
For fear this babe some day might raise again
His fallen land! Had ye so little pride?

While Hector fought, and thousands at his side,
Ye smote us, and we perished; and now, now,
When all are dead and Ilion lieth low,
Ye dread this innocent! I deem it not
Wisdom, that rage of fear that hath no thought....
   Ah, what a death hath found thee, little one!
Hadst thou but fallen fighting, hadst thou known
Strong youth and love and all the majesty
Of godlike kings, then had we spoken of thee
As of one blessed ... could in any wise
These days know blessedness. But now thine eyes
Have seen, thy lips have tasted, but thy soul
No knowledge had nor usage of the whole
Rich life that lapt thee round.... Poor little child!
Was it our ancient wall, the circuit piled
By loving Gods, so savagely hath rent
Thy curls, these little flowers innocent
That were thy mother's garden, where she laid
Her kisses; here, just where the bone-edge frayed
Grins white above—Ah heaven, I will not see!
   Ye tender arms, the same dear mould have ye
As his; how from the shoulder loose ye drop
And weak! And dear proud lips, so full of hope
And closed for ever! What false words ye said
At daybreak, when he crept into my bed,
Called me kind names, and promised: 'Grandmother,
When thou art dead, I will cut close my hair
And lead out all the captains to ride by
Thy tomb.' Why didst thou cheat me so? 'Tis I,
Old, homeless, childless, that for thee must shed
Cold tears, so young, so miserably dead.
   Dear God, the pattering welcomes of thy feet,
The nursing in my lap; and O, the sweet
Falling asleep together! All is gone.
How should a poet carve the funeral stone
To tell thy story true? 'There lieth here
A babe whom the Greeks feared, and in their fear
Slew him.' Aye, Greece will bless the tale it tells!
   Child, they have left thee beggared of all else
In Hector's house; but one thing shalt thou keep,
This war-shield bronzen-barred, wherein to sleep.
Alas, thou guardian true of Hector's fair

Left arm, how art thou masterless! And there
I see his handgrip printed on thy hold;
And deep stains of the precious sweat, that rolled
In battle from the brows and beard of him,
Drop after drop, are writ about thy rim.
    Go, bring them—such poor garments hazardous
As these days leave. God hath not granted us
Wherewith to make much pride. But all I can,
I give thee, Child of Troy.—O vain is man,
Who glorieth in his joy and hath no fears:
While to and fro the chances of the years
Dance like an idiot in the wind! And none
By any strength hath his own fortune won.

[During these lines several Women are seen approaching with garlands
    and raiment in their hands.]

LEADER.
    Lo these, who bear thee raiment harvested
    From Ilion's slain, to fold upon the dead.

[During the following scene HECUBA gradually takes the garments
    and wraps them about the Child.]

HECUBA.
    O not in pride for speeding of the car
    Beyond thy peers, not for the shaft of war
    True aimed, as Phrygians use; not any prize
    Of joy for thee, nor splendour in men's eyes,
    Thy father's mother lays these offerings
    About thee, from the many fragrant things
    That were all thine of old. But now no more.
    One woman, loathed of God, hath broke the door
    And robbed thy treasure-house, and thy warm breath
    Made cold, and trod thy people down to death!

CHORUS.

(Some Women.)

Deep in the heart of me
I feel thine hand,
Mother: and is it he
Dead here, our prince to be,
And lord of the land?

HECUBA.

Glory of Phrygian raiment, which my thought
Kept for thy bridal day with some far-sought
Queen of the East, folds thee for evermore.
And thou, grey Mother, Mother-Shield that bore
A thousand days of glory, thy last crown
Is here.... Dear Hector's shield! Thou shalt lie down
Undying with the dead, and lordlier there
Than all the gold Odysseus' breast can bear,
The evil and the strong!

CHORUS.

(Some Women.)

Child of the Shield-bearer,
Alas, Hector's child!
Great Earth, the All-mother,
Taketh thee unto her
With wailing wild!

(Others.)

Mother of misery,
Give Death his song!

(HEC. Woe!) Aye and bitterly

(HEC. Woe!) We too weep for thee,
And the infinite wrong!

[During these lines HECUBA, kneeling by the body, has been performing a funeral rite, symbolically staunching the dead Child's wounds.]

HECUBA.

I make thee whole [45];
I bind thy wounds, O little vanished soul.
This wound and this I heal with linen white:
O emptiness of aid!... Yet let the rite
Be spoken. This and.... Nay, not I, but he,
Thy father far away shall comfort thee!

[She bows her head to the ground and remains motionless and unseeing.]

CHORUS.

Beat, beat thine head:
   Beat with the wailing chime
   Of hands lifted in time:
Beat and bleed for the dead.
Woe is me for the dead!

HECUBA.

O Women! Ye, mine own....

[She rises bewildered, as though she had seen a vision.]

LEADER.

Hecuba, speak!
Thine are we all. Oh, ere thy bosom break....

HECUBA.

Lo, I have seen the open hand of God [46];
And in it nothing, nothing, save the rod
Of mine affliction, and the eternal hate,
Beyond all lands, chosen and lifted great
For Troy! Vain, vain were prayer and incense-swell
And bulls' blood on the altars!... All is well.
Had He not turned us in His hand, and thrust
Our high things low and shook our hills as dust,
We had not been this splendour, and our wrong

An everlasting music for the song
Of earth and heaven!
              Go, women: lay our dead
In his low sepulchre. He hath his meed
Of robing. And, methinks, but little care
Toucheth the tomb, if they that moulder there
Have rich encerement. 'Tis we, 'tis we,
That dream, we living and our vanity!

[The Women bear out the dead Child upon the shield, singing, when
    presently flames of fire and dim forms are seen among the ruins of
    the City.]

CHORUS.

    (Some Women.)

        Woe for the mother that bare thee, child,
          Thread so frail of a hope so high,
        That Time hath broken: and all men smiled
          About thy cradle, and, passing by,
          Spoke of thy father's majesty.
              Low, low, thou liest!

    (Others.)

        Ha! Who be these on the crested rock?
        Fiery hands in the dusk, and a shock
        Of torches flung! What lingereth still,
        O wounded City, of unknown ill,
              Ere yet thou diest?

TALTHYBIUS (coming out through the ruined Wall).
    Ye Captains that have charge to wreck this keep
    Of Priam's City, let your torches sleep
    No more! Up, fling the fire into her heart!
    Then have we done with Ilion, and may part
    In joy to Hellas from this evil land.
       And ye—so hath one word two faces—stand,
    Daughters of Troy, till on your ruined wall
    The echo of my master's trumpet call
    In signal breaks: then, forward to the sea,

    Where the long ships lie waiting.
And for thee,

O ancient woman most unfortunate,
Follow: Odysseus' men be here, and wait
To guide thee.... 'Tis to him thou go'st for thrall.

HECUBA.

    Ah, me! and is it come, the end of all,
The very crest and summit of my days?
I go forth from my land, and all its ways
Are filled with fire! Bear me, O aged feet,
A little nearer: I must gaze, and greet
My poor town ere she fall.
Farewell, farewell!

O thou whose breath was mighty on the swell
Of orient winds, my Troy! Even thy name
Shall soon be taken from thee. Lo, the flame
Hath thee, and we, thy children, pass away
To slavery.... God! O God of mercy!... Nay:
Why call I on the Gods? They know, they know,
My prayers, and would not hear them long ago.
   Quick, to the flames! O, in thine agony,
My Troy, mine own, take me to die with thee!

[She springs toward the flames, but is seized and held by the Soldiers.]

TALTHYBIUS.

    Back! Thou art drunken with thy miseries,
Poor woman!—Hold her fast, men, till it please
Odysseus that she come. She was his lot
Chosen from all and portioned. Lose her not!

[He goes to watch over the burning of the City. The dusk deepens.]

CHORUS.

(Divers Women.)

Woe, woe, woe!
Thou of the Ages [47], O wherefore fleëst thou,
Lord of the Phrygian, Father that made us?
'Tis we, thy children; shall no man aid us?
'Tis we, thy children! Seëst thou, seëst thou?

(Others.)

He seëth, only his heart is pitiless;
And the land dies: yea, she,
She of the Mighty Cities perisheth citiless!
Troy shall no more be!

(Others.)

Woe, woe, woe!
Ilion shineth afar!
Fire in the deeps thereof,
Fire in the heights above,
And crested walls of War!

(Others.)

As smoke on the wing of heaven
Climbeth and scattereth,
Torn of the spear and driven,
The land crieth for death:
O stormy battlements that red fire hath riven,
And the sword's angry breath!

[A new thought comes to HECUBA; she kneels and beats the earth with her hands.]

HECUBA.

[Strophe.]
O Earth, Earth of my children; hearken! and O mine own,
Ye have hearts and forget not, ye in the darkness lying!

LEADER.

Now hast thou found thy prayer [48], crying to them that are gone.

HECUBA.

Surely my knees are weary, but I kneel above your head;
Hearken, O ye so silent! My hands beat your bed!

LEADER.

I, I am near thee;
I kneel to thy dead to hear thee,
Kneel to mine own in the darkness; O husband, hear my crying!

HECUBA.

Even as the beasts they drive, even as the loads they bear,

LEADER.

(Pain; O pain!)

HECUBA.

We go to the house of bondage. Hear, ye dead, O hear!

LEADER.

(Go, and come not again!)

HECUBA.

Priam, mine own Priam,
Lying so lowly,
Thou in thy nothingness,
Shelterless, comfortless,
See'st thou the thing I am?
Know'st thou my bitter stress?

LEADER.

Nay, thou art naught to him!
Out of the strife there came,
Out of the noise and shame,
Making his eyelids dim,
Death, the Most Holy!

[The fire and smoke rise constantly higher.]

HECUBA.

[Antistrophe.]

O high houses of Gods, beloved streets of my birth,
Ye have found the way of the sword, the fiery and blood-red
river!

LEADER.

Fall, and men shall forget you! Ye shall lie in the gentle earth.

HECUBA.

The dust as smoke riseth; it spreadeth wide its wing;
It maketh me as a shadow, and my City a vanished thing!

LEADER.

Out on the smoke she goeth,
And her name no man knoweth;
And the cloud is northward, southward; Troy is gone for ever!

[A great crash is heard, and the Wall is lost in smoke and darkness.]

HECUBA.

Ha! Marked ye? Heard ye? The crash of the towers that fall!

LEADER.

All is gone!

HECUBA.

Wrath in the earth and quaking and a flood that sweepeth all,

LEADER.

And passeth on!

[The Greek trumpet sounds.]

HECUBA.

Farewell!—O spirit grey,
Whatso is coming,
Fail not from under me.
Weak limbs, why tremble ye?
Forth where the new long day
Dawneth to slavery!

CHORUS.
> Farewell from parting lips,
> Farewell!—Come, I and thou,
> Whatso may wait us now,
> Forth to the long Greek ships [49]
> > And the sea's foaming.

[The trumpet sounds again, and the Women go out in the darkness.]

NOTES ON THE TROJAN WOMEN

[1] Poseidon.]—In the *Iliad* Poseidon is the enemy of Troy, here the friend. This sort of confusion comes from the fact that the Trojans and their Greek enemies were largely of the same blood, with the same tribal gods. To the Trojans, Athena the War-Goddess was, of course, *their* War-Goddess, the protectress of their citadel. Poseidon, god of the sea and its merchandise, and Apollo (possibly a local shepherd god?), were their natural friends and had actually built their city wall for love of the good old king, Laomedon. Zeus, the great father, had Mount Ida for his holy hill and Troy for his peculiar city. (Cf. on p. 63.)

To suit the Greek point of view all this had to be changed or explained away. In the *Iliad* generally Athena is the proper War-Goddess of the Greeks. Poseidon had indeed built the wall for Laomedon, but Laomedon had cheated him of his reward—as afterwards he cheated Heracles, and the Argonauts and everybody else! So Poseidon hated Troy. Troy is chiefly defended by the barbarian Ares, the oriental Aphrodite, by its own rivers Scamander and Simois and suchlike inferior or unprincipled gods.

Yet traces of the other tradition remain. Homer knows that Athena is specially worshipped in Troy. He knows that Apollo, who had built the wall with Poseidon, and had the same experience of Laomedon, still loves the Trojans. Zeus himself, though eventually in obedience to destiny he permits the fall of the city, nevertheless has a great tenderness towards it.

[2] A steed marvellous.]—See below, on p. 36.

[3] I go forth from great Ilion, &c.]—The correct ancient doctrine. When your gods forsook you, there was no more hope. Conversely, when your state became desperate, evidently your gods were forsaking you. From another point of view, also, when the city was desolate and unable to worship its gods, the gods of that city were no more.

[4] Laotian Tyndarid.]—Helen was the child of Zeus and Leda, and sister of Castor and Polydeuces; but her human father was Tyndareus, an old Spartan king. She is treated as "a prisoner and a prize," *i.e.*, as a captured enemy, not as a Greek princess delivered from the Trojans.

[5] In secret slain.]—Because the Greeks were ashamed of the bloody deed. See below, p. 42, and the scene on this subject in the *Hecuba*.

[6] Cassandra.]—In the *Agamemnon* the story is more clearly told, that Cassandra was loved by Apollo and endowed by him with the

power of prophecy; then in some way she rejected or betrayed him, and he set upon her the curse that though seeing the truth she should never be believed. The figure of Cassandra in this play is not inconsistent with that version, but it makes a different impression. She is here a dedicated virgin, and her mystic love for Apollo does not seem to have suffered any breach.

[7] Pallas.]—(See above.) The historical explanation of the Trojan Pallas and the Greek Pallas is simple enough; but as soon as the two are mythologically personified and made one, there emerges just such a bitter and ruthless goddess as Euripides, in his revolt against the current mythology, loved to depict. But it is not only the mythology that he is attacking. He seems really to feel that if there are conscious gods ruling the world, they are cruel or "inhuman" beings.

[8]—Ajax the Less, son of Oïleus, either ravished or attempted to ravish Cassandra (the story occurs in both forms) while she was clinging to the Palladium or image of Pallas. It is one of the great typical sins of the Sack of Troy, often depicted on vases.

[9] Faces of ships.]—Homeric ships had prows shaped and painted to look like birds' or beasts' heads. A ship was always a wonderfully live and vivid thing to the Greek poets. (Cf. p. 64.)

[10] Castor.]—Helen's brother: the Eurôtas, the river of her home, Sparta.

[11] Fifty seeds.]—Priam had fifty children, nineteen of them children of Hecuba (*Il.* vi. 451, &c.).

[12] Pirênê.]—The celebrated spring on the hill of Corinth. Drawing water was a typical employment of slaves.

[13] ff., Theseus' land, &c.]—Theseus' land is Attica. The poet, in the midst of his bitterness over the present conduct of his city, clings the more to its old fame for humanity. The "land high-born" where the Penêüs flows round the base of Mount Olympus in northern Thessaly is one of the haunts of Euripides' dreams in many plays. Cf. *Bacchae*, 410 (p. 97 in my translation). Mount Aetna fronts the "Tyrians' citadel," *i.e.*., Carthage, built by the Phoenicians. The "sister land" is the district of Sybaris in South Italy, where the river Crathis has, or had, a red-gold colour, which makes golden the hair of men and the fleeces of sheep; and the water never lost its freshness.

[14] Talthybius is a loyal soldier with every wish to be kind. But he is naturally in good spirits over the satisfactory end of the war, and his tact is not sufficient to enable him to understand the Trojan Women's feelings. Yet in the end, since he has to see and do the cruelties which his Chiefs only order from a distance, the real nature of his work forces itself upon him, and he feels and speaks at times almost

like a Trojan. It is worth noticing how the Trojan Women generally avoid addressing him. (Cf. pp. 48, 67, 74.)

[15] The haunted keys (literally, "with God through them, penetrating them").]—Cassandra was his Key-bearer, holding the door of his Holy Place. (Cf. *Hip.* 540, p. 30.)

[16] She hath a toil, &c.]—There is something true and pathetic about this curious blindness which prevents Hecuba from understanding "so plain a riddle." (Cf. below, p. 42.) She takes the watching of a Tomb to be some strange Greek custom, and does not seek to have it explained further.

[17] Odysseus.]—In Euripides generally Odysseus is the type of the successful unscrupulous man, as soldier and politician—the incarnation of what the poet most hated. In Homer of course he is totally different.

[18] Burn themselves and die.]—Women under these circumstances did commit suicide in Euripides' day, as they have ever since. It is rather curious that none of the characters of the play, not even Andromache, kills herself. The explanation must be that no such suicide was recorded in the tradition (though cf. below, on p. 33); a significant fact, suggesting that in the Homeric age, when this kind of treatment of women captives was regular, the victims did not suffer quite so terribly under it.

[19] Hymen.]—She addresses the Torch. The shadowy Marriage-god "Hymen" was a torch and a cry as much as anything more personal. As a torch he is the sign both of marriage and of death, of sunrise and of the consuming fire. The full Moon was specially connected with marriage ceremonies.

[20] Loxias.]—The name of Apollo as an Oracular God.

[21] Cassandra's visions.]—The allusions are to the various sufferings of Odysseus, as narrated in the *Odyssey*, and to the tragedies of the house of Atreus, as told for instance in Aeschylus' *Oresteia*. Agamemnon together with Cassandra, and in part because he brought Cassandra, was murdered—felled with an axe—on his return home by his wife Clytaemnestra and her lover Aegisthus. Their bodies were cast into a pit among the rocks. In vengeance for this, Orestes, Agamemnon's son, committed "mother-murder," and in consequence was driven by the Erinyes (Furies) of his mother into madness and exile.

[22] This their king so wise.]—Agamemnon made the war for the sake of his brother Menelaus, and slew his daughter, Iphigenia, as a sacrifice at Aulis, to enable the ships to sail for Troy.

[23] Hector and Paris.]—The point about Hector is clear, but as to Paris, the feeling that, after all, it was a glory that he and the half-divine Helen loved each other, is scarcely to be found anywhere else in Greek literature. (Cf., however, Isocrates' "Praise of Helen.") Paris and Helen were never idealised like Launcelot and Guinevere, or Tristram and Iseult.

[24] A wise queen.]—Penelope, the faithful wife of Odysseus.

[25] O Heralds, yea, Voices of Death.]—There is a play on the word for "heralds" in the Greek here, which I have evaded by a paraphrase. ([Greek: Kaer-ukes] as though from [Greek: Kaer] the death-spirit, "the one thing abhorred of all mortal men.")

[26] That in this place she dies.]—The death of Hecuba is connected with a certain heap of stones on the shore of the Hellespont, called *Kunossēma*, or "Dog's Tomb." According to one tradition (Eur. *Hec.* 1259 ff.) she threw herself off the ship into the sea; according to another she was stoned by the Greeks for her curses upon the fleet; but in both she is changed after death into a sort of Hell-hound. M. Victor Bérard suggests that the dog first comes into the story owing to the accidental resemblance of the (hypothetical) Semitic word *S'qoulah*, "Stone" or "Stoning," and the Greek *Skulax*, dog. The Homeric Scylla (*Skulla*) was also both a Stone and a Dog (*Phéneciens et Odyssée*, i. 213). Of course in the present passage there is no direct reference to these wild sailor-stories.

[27] The wind comes quick.]—*i.e.*. The storm of the Prologue. Three Powers: the three Erinyes.

[28] ff., Chorus.]—The Wooden Horse is always difficult to understand, and seems to have an obscuring effect on the language of poets who treat of it. I cannot help suspecting that the story arises from a real historical incident misunderstood. Troy, we are told, was still holding out after ten years and could not be taken, until at last by the divine suggestions of Athena, a certain Epeios devised a "Wooden Horse."

What was the "device"? According to the *Odyssey* and most Greek poets, it was a gigantic wooden figure of a horse. A party of heroes, led by Odysseus, got inside it and waited. The Greeks made a show of giving up the siege and sailed away, but only as far as Tenedos. The Trojans came out and found the horse, and after wondering greatly what it was meant for and what to do with it, made a breach in their walls and dragged it into the Citadel as a thank-offering to Pallas. In the night the Greeks returned; the heroes in the horse came out and opened the gates, and Troy was captured.

It seems possible that the "device" really was the building of a wooden siege-tower, as high as the walls, with a projecting and revolving neck. Such engines were (1) capable of being used at the time in Asia, as a rare and extraordinary device, because they exist on early Assyrian monuments; (2) certain to be misunderstood in Greek legendary tradition, because they were not used in Greek warfare till many centuries later. (First, perhaps, at the sieges of Perinthus and Byzantium by Philip of Macedon, 340 B.C.)

It is noteworthy that in the great picture by Polygnôtus in the Leschê at Delphi "above the wall of Troy appears the head alone of the Wooden Horse" (*Paus.* x. 26). Aeschylus also (*Ag.* 816) has some obscure phrases pointing in the same direction: "A horse's brood, a shield-bearing people, launched with a leap about the Pleiads' setting, sprang clear above the wall," &c. Euripides here treats the horse metaphorically as a sort of war-horse trampling Troy.

[29] Her that spareth not, Heaven's yokeless rider.]—Athena like a northern Valkyrie, as often in the *Iliad*. If one tries to imagine what Athena, the War-Goddess worshipped by the Athenian mob, was like— what a mixture of bad national passions, of superstition and statecraft, of slip-shod unimaginative idealisation—one may partly understand why Euripides made her so evil. Allegorists and high-minded philosophers might make Athena entirely noble by concentrating their minds on the beautiful elements in the tradition, and forgetting or explaining away all that was savage; he was determined to pin her down to the worst facts recorded of her, and let people worship such a being if they liked!

[30] To Artemis.]—Maidens at the shrine of Artemis are a fixed datum in the tradition. (Cf. *Hec.* 935 ff.)

[31] Andromache and Hecuba.]—This very beautiful scene is perhaps marred to most modern readers by an element which is merely a part of the convention of ancient mourning. Each of the mourners cries: "There is no affliction like mine!" and then proceeds to argue, as it were, against the other's counter claim. One can only say that it was, after all, what they expected of each other; and I believe the same convention exists in most places where keening or wailing is an actual practice.

[32] Even as the sound of a song.]—I have filled in some words which seem to be missing in the Greek here.

[33] Andromache.]—This character is wonderfully studied. She seems to me to be a woman who has not yet shown much character or perhaps had very intense experience, but is only waiting for sufficiently great trials to become a heroine and a saint. There is still a marked

element of conventionality in her description of her life with Hector; but one feels, as she speaks, that she is already past it. Her character is built up of "*Sophrosyne*," of self-restraint and the love of goodness— qualities which often seem second-rate or even tiresome until they have a sufficiently great field in which to act. Very characteristic is her resolution to make the best, and not the worst, of her life in Pyrrhus' house, with all its horror of suffering and apparent degradation. So is the self-conquest by which she deliberately refrains from cursing her child's murderers, for the sake of the last poor remnant of good she can still do to him, in getting him buried. The nobility of such a character depends largely, of course, on the intensity of the feelings conquered.

It is worth noting, in this connection, that Euripides is contradicting a wide-spread tradition (Robert, *Bild und Lied*, pp. 63 ff.). Andromache, in the pictures of the Sack of Troy, is represented with a great pestle or some such instrument fighting with the Soldiers to rescue Astyanax ([Greek: 'Andro-machae] = "Man-fighting").

Observe, too, what a climax of drama is reached by means of the very fact that Andromache, to the utmost of her power, tries to do nothing "dramatic," but only what will be best. Her character in Euripides' play, *Andromache*, is, on the whole, similar to this, but less developed.

[34] In Salamis, filled with the foaming, &c.]—A striking instance of the artistic value of the Greek chorus in relieving an intolerable strain. The relief provided is something much higher than what we ordinarily call "relief"; it is a stream of pure poetry and music in key with the sadness of the surrounding scene, yet, in a way, happy just because it is beautiful. (Cf. note on *Hippolytus*, 1. 732.)

The argument of the rather difficult lyric is: "This is not the first time Troy has been taken. Long ago Heracles made war against the old king Laomedon, because he had not given him the immortal steeds that he promised. And Telamon joined him; Telamon who might have been happy in his island of Salamis, among the bees and the pleasant waters, looking over the strait to the olive-laden hills of Athens, the beloved City! And they took ship and slew Laomedon. Yea, twice Zeus has destroyed Ilion!

(Second part.) Is it all in vain that our Trojan princes have been loved by the Gods? Ganymêdês pours the nectar of Zeus in his banquets, his face never troubled, though his motherland is burned with fire! And, to say nothing of Zeus, how can the Goddess of Morning rise and shine upon us uncaring? She loved Tithônus, son of Laomedon, and bore him up from us in a chariot to be her husband in the skies. But all that once made them love us is gone!"

[35] Pools of thy bathing.]—It is probable that Ganymêdês was himself originally a pool or a spring on Ida, now a pourer of nectar in heaven.

[36] Menelaus and Helen.]—The meeting of Menelaus and Helen after the taking of Troy was naturally one of the great moments in the heroic legend. The versions, roughly speaking, divide themselves into two. In one (*Little Iliad*, Ar. *Lysistr.* 155, Eur. *Andromache* 628) Menelaus is about to kill her, but as she bares her bosom to the sword, the sword falls from his hand. In the other (Stesichorus, *Sack of Ilion* (?)) Menelaus or some one else takes her to the ships to be stoned, and the men cannot stone her. As Quintus of Smyrna says, "They looked on her as they would on a God!"

Both versions have affected Euripides here. And his Helen has just the magic of the Helen of legend. That touch of the supernatural which belongs of right to the Child of Heaven—a mystery, a gentleness, a strange absence of fear or wrath—is felt through all her words. One forgets to think of her guilt or innocence; she is too wonderful a being to judge, too precious to destroy. This supernatural element, being the thing which, if true, separates Helen from other women, and in a way redeems her, is for that reason exactly what Hecuba denies. The controversy has a certain eternal quality about it: the hypothesis of heavenly enchantment and the hypothesis of mere bad behaviour, neither of them entirely convincing! But the very curses of those that hate her make a kind of superhuman atmosphere about Helen in this play; she fills the background like a great well-spring of pain.

This Menelaus, however, is rather different from the traditional Menelaus. Besides being the husband of Helen, he is the typical Conqueror, for whose sake the Greeks fought and to whom the central prize of the war belongs. And we take him at the height of his triumph, the very moment for which he made the war! Hence the peculiar bitterness with which he is treated, his conquest turning to ashes in his mouth, and his love a confused turmoil of hunger and hatred, contemptible and yet terrible.

The exit of the scene would leave a modern audience quite in doubt as to what happened, unless the action were much clearer than the words. But all Athenians knew from the *Odyssey* that the pair were swiftly reconciled, and lived happily together as King and Queen of Sparta.

[37] Thou deep base of the world.]—These lines, as a piece of religious speculation, were very famous in antiquity. And dramatically they are most important. All through the play Hecuba is a woman of remarkable intellectual power and of fearless thought. She does not

definitely deny the existence of the Olympian gods, like some characters in Euripides, but she treats them as beings that have betrayed her, and whose name she scarcely deigns to speak. It is the very godlessness of Hecuba's fortitude that makes it so terrible and, properly regarded, so noble. (Cf. p. 35 "Why call on things so weak?" and p. 74 "They know, they know....") Such Gods were as a matter of fact the moral inferiors of good men, and Euripides will never blind his eyes to their inferiority. And as soon as people see that their god is bad, they tend to cease believing in his existence at all. (Hecuba's answer to Helen is not inconsistent with this, it is only less characteristic.)

Behind this Olympian system, however, there is a possibility of some real Providence or impersonal Governance of the world, to which here, for a moment, Hecuba makes a passionate approach. If there is *any* explanation, *any* justice, even in the form of mere punishment of the wicked, she will be content and give worship! But it seems that there is not. Then at last there remains—what most but not all modern freethinkers would probably have begun to doubt at the very beginning—the world of the departed, the spirits of the dead, who are true, and in their dim way love her still (p. 71 "Thy father far away shall comfort thee," and the last scene of the play).

This last religion, faint and shattered by doubt as it is, represents a return to the most primitive "Pelasgian" beliefs, a worship of the Dead which existed long before the Olympian system, and has long outlived it.

[38] The fire-brand's image.]—Hecuba, just before Paris' birth, dreamed that she gave birth to a fire-brand. The prophets therefore advised that the babe should be killed; but Priam disobeyed them.

[39] Three Crowns of Life.]—On the Judgment of Paris see Miss Harrison, *Prolegomena*. pp. 292 ff. Late writers degrade the story into a beauty contest between three thoroughly personal goddesses—and a contest complicated by bribery. But originally the Judgment is rather a Choice between three possible lives, like the Choice of Heracles between Work and Idleness. The elements of the choice vary in different versions: but in general Hera is royalty; Athena is prowess in war or personal merit; Aphrodite, of course, is love. And the goddesses are not really to be distinguished from the gifts they bring. They are what they give, and nothing more. Cf. the wonderful lyric *Androm.* 274 ff., where they come to "a young man walking to and fro alone, in an empty hut in the firelight."

There is an extraordinary effect in Helen herself *being* one of the Crowns of Life—a fair equivalent for the throne of the world.

[40] Alexander ... Paris.]—Two plays on words in the Greek.

[41] The old Gate-Warden.]—He and the Watchers are, of course, safely dead. But on the general lines of the tradition it may well be that Helen is speaking the truth. She loved both Menelaus and Paris; and, according to some versions, hated Dêiphobus, the Trojan prince who seized her after Paris' death. There is a reference to Dêiphobus in the MSS. of the play here, but I follow Wilamowitz in thinking it spurious.

[42] Chorus.]—On the Trojan Zeus see above, on p. 11. Mount Ida caught the rays of the rising sun in some special manner and distributed them to the rest of the world; and in this gleam of heavenly fire the God had his dwelling, which is now the brighter for the flames of his City going up like incense!

Nothing definite is known of the Golden Images and the Moon-Feasts.

[43] Towers of the Giants.]—The pre-historic castles of Tiryns and Mycênae.

[44] May Helen be there.]—(Cf. above.) Pitanê was one of the five divisions of Sparta. Athena had a "Bronzen House" on the acropolis of Sparta. Simoïs, of course, the river of Troy.

[45] I make thee whole.]—Here as elsewhere Hecuba fluctuates between fidelity to the oldest and most instinctive religion, and a rejection of all Gods.

[46] Lo, I have seen the open hand of God.]—The text is, perhaps, imperfect here; but Professor Wilamowitz agrees with me that Hecuba has seen something like a vision. The meaning of this speech is of the utmost importance. It expresses the inmost theme of the whole play, a search for an answer to the injustice of suffering in the very splendour and beauty of suffering. Of course it must be suffering of a particular kind, or, what comes to the same thing, suffering borne in a particular way; but in that case the answer seems to me to hold. One does not really think the world evil because there are martyrs or heroes in it. For them the elements of beauty which exist in any great trial of the spirit become so great as to overpower the evil that created them—to turn it from shame and misery into tragedy. Of course to most sufferers, to children and animals and weak people, or those without inspiration, the doctrine brings no help. It is a thing invented by a poet for himself.

[47] Thou of the Ages.]—The Phrygian All-Father, identified with Zeus, son of Kronos. (Cf. on p. 11.)

[48] Now hast thou found thy prayer.]—The Gods have deserted her, but she has still the dead. (Cf. above, on p. 71.)

[49] Forth to the dark Greek ships.]—Curiously like another magnificent ending of a great poem, that of the *Chanson de Roland*, where Charlemagne is called forth on a fresh quest:

"Deus," dist li Reis, "si penuse est ma vie!"
Pluret des oilz, sa barbe blanche tiret....

THE END

Printed in the United States
80505LV00001B/59

9 781420 927320